Made in the USA
Coppell, TX
03 May 2022

77365683R00057